Read About
Johnny Appleseed

Stephen Feinstein

Enslow Elementary
an imprint of
Enslow Publishers, Inc.

40 Industrial Road   PO Box 38
Box 398   Aldershot
Berkeley Heights, NJ 07922   Hants GU12 6BP
USA   UK
http://www.enslow.com

Words to Know

cellars—Underground rooms used for storage.

crop—Plants grown for food.

orchard—A place where fruit trees are grown.

Revolutionary War—The war between England and America from 1775 to 1783. After the war, the United States of America was a separate country.

settlers—People who move to a new place.

wilderness—Land with no farms or towns.

Enslow Elementary, an imprint of Enslow Publishers, Inc.

Enslow Elementary® is a registered trademark of Enslow Publishers, Inc.

Copyright © 2006 by Enslow Publishers, Inc.

All rights reserved.

No part of this book may be reproduced by any means without the written permission of the publisher.

Library of Congress Cataloging-in-Publication Data

Feinstein, Stephen.
  Read about Johnny Appleseed / Stephen Feinstein.
    p. cm. — (I like biographies!)
  Includes bibliographical references and index.
  ISBN 0-7660-2599-3
  1. Appleseed, Johnny, 1774–1845—Juvenile literature. 2. Apple growers—United States—Biography—Juvenile literature. 3. Frontier and pioneer life—Middle West—Juvenile literature. I. Title. II. Series.
  SB63.C46F45 2006
  634'.11092—dc22
       [B]
                          2005025573

Printed in the United States of America

10 9 8 7 6 5 4 3 2 1

To Our Readers: We have done our best to make sure all Internet Addresses in this book were active and appropriate when we went to press. However, the author and the publisher have no control over and assume no liability for the material available on those Internet sites or on links to other Web sites. Any comments or suggestions can be sent by e-mail to comments@enslow.com or to the address on the back cover.

Every effort has been made to locate all copyright holders of material used in this book. If any errors or omissions have occurred, corrections will be made in future editions.

Illustration Credits: Courtesy of Allen County/Fort Wayne Historical Society, pp. 1, 15; Courtesy of American Antiquarian Society, p. 9; AP/Wide World, p. 21; Artville, LLC/Enslow Publishers, Inc., p. 19; Clipart.com, p. 22; Corel Corp., p. 7; Library of Congress, p. 5; National Park Service, p. 13; North Wind Picture Archives, p. 17; Photos.com, pp. 3, 11.

Cover Illustration: John Hancock Insurance Co.

Contents

1 Alone in the Woods 4

2 In the Apple Orchard 8

3 Johnny Goes West 12

4 Johnny Gets a New Name 16

Timeline 22

Learn More 23

Index 24

Chapter 1
Alone in the Woods

John Chapman, who later became known as Johnny Appleseed, was born in Massachusetts on September 26, 1774. When Johnny was two, his father, Nathaniel, went off to fight the British in the **Revolutionary War**. Shortly after, Johnny's mother and baby brother became ill and died. Johnny and his sister, Elizabeth, went to live with their grandparents.

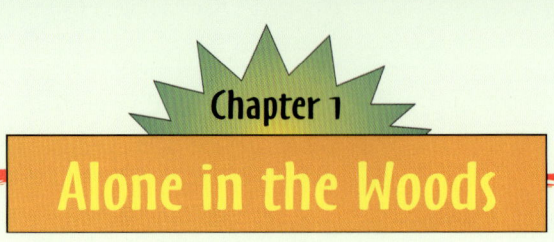

John Chapman became famous for planting apple trees.

When Johnny was six, his father returned from the war and married a woman named Lucy. Johnny and Elizabeth went to live at their new farm. As the years went by, Nathaniel and Lucy raised ten more children.

Johnny liked playing with his brothers and sisters. But most of all he loved exploring the nearby woods. It was peaceful and quiet in the forest.

Johnny was happy to be alone with nature. He felt most at home in the woods.

Chapter 2
In the Apple Orchard

While he was growing up, Johnny learned about apples. The Chapmans and their neighbors grew apple trees. The apple was a very important **crop** for farm families. They stored apples in their **cellars** so that they could have fruit to eat all through the winter. People also used apples to make applesauce, apple cider, apple pies, apple butter, and vinegar.

This picture shows a farmer making apple cider. The horse is turning a machine that presses the juice out of the apples.

Every year in the fall, Johnny would help his father pick apples in the **orchard**. Johnny was just as happy in the orchard as he was in the woods. He was always amazed to see how the beautiful white apple blossoms in the spring became red ripe apples by the fall.

These pictures show an apple tree with blossoms in the spring and apples in the fall.

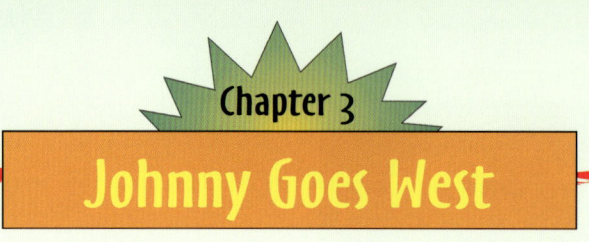

Chapter 3
Johnny Goes West

In 1797, Johnny was twenty-three. At this time, white **settlers** were moving west across Indian lands. They cleared land in the forest and built log cabins.

Johnny liked the idea of building his own log cabin. He knew he would be happy in the woods.

Settlers who moved west built log cabins like this one.

Johnny had a plan. He would move west and find some good land. Then he would build a house and plant apple trees.

Johnny said goodbye to his family and started walking west. He carried a sack of apple seeds. He kept walking until he reached the western part of Pennsylvania.

Johnny loved animals, and he was happy living in the woods.

Chapter 4
Johnny Gets a New Name

Johnny planted his apple seeds in the rich soil of the **wilderness**. Soon he finished planting his first apple orchard. Johnny then started more orchards in other parts of the forest.

The Indians respected Johnny because of his love for nature. They taught him many useful things to help him live in the wilderness.

Some drawings show Johnny wearing a cooking pot on his head. In this picture, though, his hat is made of cardboard.

When Johnny ran out of apple seeds, he went back east for more. In a few years, Johnny began selling his young apple trees to the settlers. They began to call him Johnny Appleseed.

In 1804, Johnny moved further west to Ohio, planting apple seeds all over the wilderness. By now he had so many apple trees that he often gave them away.

This map shows how far Johnny walked to plant trees. The lines show some of the places he may have traveled.

In 1845, Johnny got sick while walking through a snowstorm in Indiana. He died on March 18.

Today, apples still grow on some of the trees that Johnny planted. We will always remember Johnny Appleseed for his hard work and gentle life.

Johnny Appleseed is still famous today. Here is a Johnny Appleseed balloon in a parade.

Timeline

1774—Johnny is born in Leominster, Massachusetts, on September 26.

1776—Johnny's father leaves to fight in the war. His mother dies. Johnny and his sister, Elizabeth, go to live with their grandparents.

1780—Johnny and Elizabeth go to live with their father and stepmother.

1797—Johnny walks west to Pennsylvania.

1804—Johnny moves further west to Ohio.

1845—Johnny dies near Fort Wayne, Indiana, on March 18.

Learn More

Books

Gibbons, Gail. *Apples*. New York: Holiday House, 2000.

Kurtz, Jane. *Johnny Appleseed*. New York: Aladdin Paperbacks, 2004.

Schaefer, Lola M. *Johnny Appleseed*. Mankato, Minn.: Pebble Books, 2003.

Web Sites

"Johnny Appleseed"
<http://www.appleappetite.com/Johnny.htm>

"The Story of Johnny Appleseed"
<http://www.applejuice.org/johnnyappleseed.html>

Index

apples, 8, 10, 14, 16, 18, 20

Chapman, Elizabeth, 4, 6

Chapman, John
    childhood, 4, 6, 8, 10
    death, 20
    moves west, 14, 18
    plants apple trees, 16, 18, 20

Chapman, Lucy, 4

Chapman, Nathaniel, 4, 6, 10

Indiana, 20

Indians, 12, 16

Johnny Appleseed. *See* Chapman, John.

Massachusetts, 4

Ohio, 18

Pennsylvania, 14

Revolutionary War, 4

settlers, 12

FEB 17 2010
21-26